Hope
You
Don't
Get
Famous

Poetry & Prose

Hope You Don't Get Famous

Vernajh E. Pinder

Printed in the United States of America

First Printing, October 2019

ISBN 978-1-6928-6333-3

Illustrations: Abdul Mannan Mokhtar
Book Cover: Shmaelgraphics

Second Edition

Hope
You
Don't
Get
Famous

Poetry & Prose

For A.D C.C, J.A, J.H & K.A, thanks for showing me that true love existed. To S.F, this is just the beginning.

To all the individuals I have loved before, it stops now.

Introduction

Dear heartbreak,

This book describes the actual story of what happened and not the false narrative you have decided to write for your name's sake. I refuse to let you sell your lies to the highest bidder because there are always two sides to every story, yours and the truth. For too long, I have sat back and listened as you slandered and dragged my name through the mud. And all for what? So, you can get a leg up? So, you can fill the emptiness inside of you? Well, no more! I have come to wrest sovereignty from your vile, iniquitous clutch. Your reign has ended, and I will reclaim the throne that is rightfully mine.

I fell for your façade and mistook it for me. The depths of your soul manipulated me into believing you were beautiful when it was revolting. I wanted to believe you were a caterpillar evolving into a butterfly. Instead, you were a Venus Fly Trap trying to confine me to anguish. Eventually, I stopped striving to see the beauty in you and accepted you for the sadist you are. To believe that I let you deceive me is unbecoming.

However, you have reached the end of your rope. I bid thee farewell. I have romanticized you for far too long. The glory you want is not coming anymore. You have wreaked too much havoc in my name, and just for attention. So, in the end, I hope you don't get famous. And honestly, I will make sure of it.

Love,

Love

Section One

I loved you before I even loved myself. Everything I should have poured into who I wanted to become, I emptied into you. The idea of the love story that could have been becoming the object of my obsession and at that point, nothing else in my life mattered, only you.

I'm still the kid

that believes in

happily ever after

and no one can

convince me otherwise

There his heart sat
on display for everyone
to poke and prude,
to gawk at.
Everything he spent
his entire life guarding
was out in the open
for the whole world
to pick apart
and leave him in pieces,
as they casually
steal parts of him
to keep for themselves.
Even though they say
he was never good enough.

Flowers bloom,

but trees grow.

Why can't love bloom like trees,

will my heart ever know?

The door opened
and when I look inside
to see the sunrise,
in those moments,
I finally knew
it would be you
who had become the sun
in which my world
would never revolve around

Like the roots of a tree,

my love for you deepens

Kiss me

and let the wind

carry our love

in the breeze

Vernajh Pinder

Dear love,

I met someone today.

I thought it was you,

but it appeared to be another imposter.

Can I meet you soon?

Sincerely,

The Heart

There once was a guy, twenty,

who fell in love with so many

he left with a bruise

cause wrong he would choose

and now the guy's heart? Empty

I close my eyes,

and I count to three.

I open them wide,

it's you I see.

the girl of my dreams

although it seems,

I'm not the man

you need me to be

There she stood confidently,

as I approached her gradually.

Her aura like no other.

It was then that I knew,

with her, I wanted to

spend the rest of my life.

Simple rhythm,

perfect pitch

beautiful melodies

sounds so rich

Sounds so rich,

eager tones

gliding keys,

metronome

Metronome,

piercing falsettos

radiant beams,

voices mellow

voices mellow

soulful ballads

creeping tempo

exquisite palate

exquisite palate,

harmony fading

equal climax,

blissful cadence

It seems that the pain I subjected you to

was sometimes too much to bear

and like a circle, you reciprocated.

The constant ebbing and flowing

and then never knowing

what's next in the story

of this love between you and me.

But is this love?

It seems we somehow misinterpreted it.

The love you gave to me was all I have ever gotten.

I still don't comprehend what it should feel like,

but whatever it is I sense when I'm with you

I don't ever want not to feel it.

Even if it isn't real

So, say you'll never leave

Just say you won't let go

I remember the nights
when I could only think about you.
The way your breath felt
when it would intertwine with mine.

It's the little things I remember
Like when we first met
 you couldn't pronounce my name.
Oh, how time flies
because now every time you say it,
it drives me insane.

My love for you transcends

anything this world will

throw at us

As we lay here

I replay our most

intimate moments.

The way our bodies would move

with a mind of their own.

The way our limbs

tangled, untangled, and tangled again

The way your lips emitted heat,

to every nook of my body.

The ways in which

you made me feel whole.

But especially the way

your tender "I love you,"

danced on the inside of my ear.

It is in these moments

I'm reminded

of just how much

you mean to me,

and how much I'm

willing to fight for us

until I draw my last breath.

and even after

I will still be fighting

for us in the next.

I trace your body

like I play each key.

The rhythm to my harmony

the tempo to each beat.

Written with passion,

scars on the soul.

A rest in each measure,

from quarters to halves, to wholes.

Our love a chord,

in perfect form.

Each stroke of beauty,

the sound of the norm.

Together our melodies,

gently intertwine.

A piece so perfect,

transcending through time.

Without a final word,

love packed its bags

and went away.

Leaving the heart

heartbroken,

with nothing to fill its place.

This felt safe at first.

Our love was gentle,

 and you stole my heart

like a thief in the night.

I was happy that you did

because we were happy then.

Our happiness felt like a bubble,

one that was indestructible,

and during that period,

everything was good.

It was picturesque, honestly.

Then, as if on impulse,

everything gradually began to fall apart.

I watched petrified

as we wafted away from each other,

having to observe you

becoming someone new.

Each day that

I would gaze in your eyes,

I was hoping that

the person I once loved

had somehow survived.

Unfortunately, you didn't

and that's how it all started,

when you irreversibly became

the brute you were destined to be.

Poetry is art

and to me, art

is the abstract representation

of everything you mean to me,

of everything you make me feel.

Therefore, you are my poetry.

Tell me you don't love me
so I can walk away.
Let me leave
so my heart doesn't break.
Don't lead me on,
don't drag this out.
I'm hurting
and I don't know
how much more I can take.
So, tell me you don't want me
and I'll walk away

The wind whipped
the insolence
out of the sun,
replacing it
with the civility
of the moon,
leaving the clouds
in awe
and the stars
speechless.

Section Two

When someone reveals who they genuinely are to you, don't look away. You must force yourself to confront that reality, no matter how dreadful it gets. You cannot continue to excuse their behavior and make it okay. When will enough be enough? At what point do the excuses stop and the accountability happen?

Hope You Don't Get Famous
.

Maybe I am just

a hopeless romantic,

wishing you could feel

the love my heart has

lying in wait for you.

The pain danced
around in her heart
as she replayed in her mind
all the men
that hurt her before,
that left her aching and lonely,
trapped in a never-ending cycle.
She wanted so bad for
someone to come and love her,
but she knew that
she would have to love herself
a little more first

Hope You Don't Get Famous

With a knife,
I let you write
on my heart
leaving scars
that seem like
they will never heal

Vernajh Pinder

There sat a beautiful
house on the hill
filled with deception and lies.
There in the city,
an exterior so pretty
that he ever realized.
As he opened the door
and maneuvered the floor
that he was going to die
So, there he lied
on the bed of lies
all wrapped in disguise
and hidden behind her eyes.

Hope You Don't Get Famous

The moon cries in agony
as the sun begins its ascent
to give light to the world
and set us free
from the darkness
the moon cast.

I watched as you walked away
without a second glance.
You packed up and left my place,
didn't give me a second chance
I gave my whole life to you,
at least that's how it feels.
I invested so much in our love,
a love I thought was real.
We spent many nights
entwined in each other's arms.
Life was three worlds away
because you were safe here in my arms.
Still, you left me broken
over something so taboo.
I couldn't help the fact
that I'm in love with you

She loved you

with all the broken

parts of herself

and you loved her

wholeheartedly.

Hope You Don't Get Famous

He wrote multiple love letters
hoping you would respond,
but you never did
and he often wondered
why you didn't love him.

I light up your world like the sun does the earth.
I move mountains for you, yet you treat me like dirt
I quench your thirst by purifying the sea
I did all that, and you still left me?

Hope You Don't Get Famous

Typically, a caterpillar turns

into a butterfly

but is it a lie?

In my mind, you were the caterpillar

that never morphed into a butterfly

because butterflies are beautiful

but you, you are a monster.

Vernajh Pinder

There once was a girl, one
whose aura shined like the sun.
She glittered like gold,
but her heart was cold
so if you love her, run

There once was a girl with no soul
whose heart was as black as coal.
She fell on a knife,
it ended her life
and the girl with no soul was cold.

Vernajh Pinder

My mind wandered like the branches of a tree
as it lingered with thoughts of you and me
my heart ached, my spirit was cracked
because I couldn't seem to get over the fact,
that we were finished, over and done
that the war was over, the battle was won
you broke my soul, and you hurt me bad
I lost who I was, became so mad
consumed with anger, coupled with grief
then came the depression, the disbelief
I loved you so deeply that my heart would convulse

but you left me dead, my body no pulse.

Hope You Don't Get Famous

The darkness
swallowed him whole
and he was trapped
with no escape in sight.

My love for you was like magic.
You never knew it was real
until you felt it
and once you did,
you never stopped believing.

Hope You Don't Get Famous

The world seemed different, a little hollow.
I was drenched in agony, cemented in sorrow.
You left me there, with no thoughts of tomorrow.
You took my time because you take not borrow.

The roses died as my soul did wither,
and just like a snake, you hiss and slither.
The judas kiss, you're such a good kisser.
Without a trace, you were faint like a whisper

So now I'm sinking, falling blindly
you ripped my heart out of my chest,
and you took the best parts of me
leaving a gaping hole with nothing to fill it.

Ashes of your love

floated on the breeze

and he danced carefreely.

He danced as the ashes

of your love

fell from the heavens.

The wind howled; the trees danced.

Like the stars at night, my heart twinkled.

The sun sunk; the night glowed.

The thunder spoke, my heart kindled.

The lightning ran. The leaves spun.

My thoughts stayed as my mind run.

The sky burst. Followed by my heart.

The waves sang. The moon barked.

As I tried desperately to rekindle the spark.

The poles stared. The roots giggled.

A joke to them. My heart is fickle.

The flowers bowed. The rain attacked

My heartbreak made them go, "Clap, Clap, Clap."

The grass stung—the darkness bicker.

My heart to you broke, no elixir.

Vernajh Pinder

He wore his heart
on his sleeve,
but instead of protecting it
you chose to throw knives at it.

Hope You Don't Get Famous

I ransacked

every inch of

your soul

hoping

to find

the girl

I once loved,

only to understand

that the girl

I loved

never existed.

She just wanted the love
her father never gave
her mother,
but she couldn't tell you
what that would even look like.

Hope You Don't Get Famous

Her eyes held the secrets

that her soul

attempted to hide away,

you just never looked deep enough.

Vernajh Pinder

He would always
see your reflection
in the glass of wine
and in those moments
he felt closer to you,
so he would keep drinking.

Hope You Don't Get Famous

Everyone told him

you would never love him.

Despite this,

he was still willing

to take the risk.

Section Three

Thoughts of you continue to implode my mind. Feelings that can't be washed away by the rain. It's like, although I've finally gotten to a point where I think I'm over you, the sound of the rain always brings you back. It's interesting how simple moments can bring a flood of memories rushing back in.

Hope You Don't Get Famous

I became so obsessed
with the idea of you
because of the temporary
nirvana you made me feel,
I had never felt it before.
So when I finally felt it with you
I held onto it
because this high was everything.
However, as much as I'd like to
be high off this idea of
you and me,
I can't continue to force
this illusion.
Maybe in another life
we would have worked out
but in this one, we won't
and I must find the peace
within myself
to be okay with that.

Vernajh Pinder

Sometimes the only way
to get healing
is to forgive yourself
and let go of the things
stopping you from making progress.

Hope You Don't Get Famous

She threw paint
wildly against the canvas.
The result was
an abstract portrait
glistening with beauty.

Vernajh Pinder

I hope your tires get flat
and your life turns blue.
I hope your hair falls out
and you don't know what to do.
I hope your peace gets stolen
and your happiness goes missing.
I hope you call around for help,
but nobody will listen.
I hope your heart gets broken,
for each time you broke mine.
I hope it hurts like hell,
and you can't stop crying.
I hope your world falls apart,
crumbles, turns upside down.
I hope you lose everything that you love.
Hell; I hope your house burns to the ground
I hope your karma is relentless,
and I pray one day you read this.
Most of all, I hope in my heart,
I hope you don't get famous.

Vernajh Pinder

Loneliness is grey

and heavy is the weight

in which it suffocates me.

A reminder that,

though colors come on a spectrum,

grey is the only color

that continues to look good on me.

Hope You Don't Get Famous

The pain pressed against his chest,
like an elephant standing on a peanut.
He could hear his rib cage shatter
the more the pressure was applied

Each bone a missile
that seemed to be aimed at his heart.
He felt the invigorating pain
as each bone pierced through his heart,
one explosion after the other.

They say that love comes from the heart.
So, did this mean he loved himself?
With each ounce of blood leaving his body,
was it love filling his body?

Like a drug addict,
he was fiending for love, always craving it.
As he drew his final breaths
he couldn't help feeling a pang of regret
because he wore his heart on his sleeve
for everyone to see
and aim at.

Vernajh Pinder

I would always envision us
sitting on a balcony in Paris.
Inhabiting a space of our own
that overlooked the Eiffel.
We would drink coffee
and watch as the sun
would set in the distance
but it seems
 the only place the sun
is only setting on our love.

Hope You Don't Get Famous

You said, " you craved my existence."
It's funny how I only existed
when you needed
to get high on intimacy.

Vernajh Pinder

I could feel the discord
like you played the wrong key
as my anger crept up adagio
I can't believe the beat to which you played me
and just like that, my rage rose to a crescendo.
You whispered in my ear
and you told me that you love me,
my lips to yours meet
as I get ready for my soliloquy.

It was then you put the ensemble together,
and entirely on cue, you plucked the strings.
The melody was played in my unholy disaster.
I knew then that I was just a piece
and that this measure was for your entertainment,
so the F was sharp in my resentment

Isn't it a bit crazy
that the moment
you reverted to a
mere memory in
my head, you told
me you loved me,
and without me,
you're incomplete?

Vernajh Pinder

I waited seven years for you,

and you never came.

Instead, two years later, you came,

but it wasn't the same.

So, I bid thee farewell,

and I hope you find

someone just like you,

and they give you hell.

Hope You Don't Get Famous

He bought her a house,
he gave her some flowers.
He gave all his love,
investing so many hours.

She accepted his gifts
while he held her tight.
Yet, in the back of her mind,
she knew what she was doing wasn't right

He kissed her lovingly.
He caressed her body.
She broke his heart.
His world now cloudy

He cried for hours,
he didn't eat for days.
He never left his room,
he was in a broken phase.

She knew what she'd done,
somehow, she didn't even care.
She'd already moved on,
the next man was there.

Vernajh Pinder

He saw them together,
he broke on the inside.
His head started spinning,
those feelings he did not hide

She smiled on the inside
not knowing what she'd done
she felt so much power
thinking she'd won

He went to his room
and closed the door.
He put the gun to his head
and felt no more.

She laid there bleeding,
trying to catch her breath.
She thought she'd be happy,
but the new guy beat her to death.

Hope You Don't Get Famous

Every time she cried,

he would kiss the tears

from her eyes

and whisper,

"I got you.

It's all going to be okay."

Vernajh Pinder

Beautiful puddles,
streams of lies.
Heartbreak and torment,
open eyes.

Alcohol numbing,
imperfection.
Morphine, cocaine,
simple addiction.

Hospital visits,
get well soon.
Dressed in all black,
gone too soon.

Societal approval,
held too high.
Fall ten times,
get up nine

My eyes are red,
my heart is full.
My pain is real,
tears are beautiful.

Blood boiling, hellbent.
Dressed in scars, heaven-sent.
Lightly washed, gentle care.
Lay it out, naked, bare

Open gashes, nasty wounds.
Racing thoughts, adjacent rooms.
Faint whispers, chilling breeze.
Loose grips, I'm begging you, please.

Broken heart, blue eyes.
Bruised soul, pleading cries.
Web of lies, smoke, and mirrors.
Giving love? A common error.

Bloody gowns, last dance.
A sacred ritual, no chance.
Aeroplane, needle vein.
No heartbeat, cellophane.

Hope You Don't Get Famous

I tried to put it

all in words

so I could write

a letter,

but I couldn't

find the right words

to tell you

how much you

I hate you.

So, instead, I

just left.

We were supposed to change
the world together,
but instead
you changed the rules
and that didn't make
it any better
because in the end
you look like a fool.

Hope You Don't Get Famous

My happiness has always
found its voice
when the rain brewed.
It's like the sun,
yellow in awe,
could never give me
the same feelings
compared to the grey of the rain.
Needless to say, you are my rain

I think the worst part about it
is that I gave you my all
and you didn't reciprocate,
you purposely let me fall.

I invested my time into you.
I put your needs above mine
yet, with pure consistency,
you let me down each time.

It seems that I was insane
for thinking you'd change
but in the end
you'd always stay the same.

Maybe it was me honestly,
I just couldn't fathom
the fact that,
no matter what I do,
I'll never have you back.

Hope You Don't Get Famous

My mind can't seem to wrap itself
around this idea
that we aren't meant
to be together.
The thought eludes me
seeking shelter in a safe place,
the sanctuary where only you and I exist,
the place where we are together,
the corners of my mind

It seems like it was just yesterday,

that I was willing to risk it all.

Like the ebb and flow of the tide,

you washed away everything I felt.

So, now I feel nothing

and I don't know what hurts more,

losing the illusion of who you were

or accepting the integrity of who you are.

Hope You Don't Get Famous

Before you walkout

and leave me for good,

sit with me for a moment.

Look me in the eye

and lie to me.

Tell me that you love me

one last time,

and then you can leave.

Vernajh Pinder

There he stood
watching as the rain
washed away everything
he had spent his life building.
In an instant
he was left with nothing.

Hope You Don't Get Famous

You are everything I always wanted,
but I ended up with something
I didn't deserve

- heartbreak

Section Four

The first step for us to make progress of any kind is to be honest with our intentions. Honest,y no matter how much it hurts, sets the foundation. If you add lies or half-truths to it, you get cracks in the surface. These cracks now allow anything to permeate. So, eventually, the foundation crumbles.

Hope You Don't Get Famous

The essence of your soul
was so remarkably beautiful
that no matter the penalty
I would move every single planet,
if that meant we could be together.

Hope You Don't Get Famous

I became so obsessed
with the idea of you
because the temporary
nirvana you made me feel,
I had never felt it before
so, when I finally felt it with you
I held onto it
because this high was everything.
However, as much as I'd like to
be high off this idea of
you and me,
I can't continue to force
this illusion
that one day we'll work out.
We won't
and I must find the peace
within myself
to be okay with that.

Each day

you fade away

brings my heart

closer to inner peace.

She was afraid to love him

because everything

she had loved,

she lost.

Before you leave forever
allow me one more day
to love you.
Only then will I be done
holding onto the
nothing that exists.

The hardest thing for me to
wrap my mind around was
your willingness to love me
when I wasn't willing to love myself.
Thank you!

Sometimes we fall

in love with

the right person

at the wrong time.

Everyone deserves

a second chance

Hope You Don't Get Famous

I'd rather spend my time
being mad at you.
To be angry
about the messed-up about things you do.
I'd rather say I hate you
instead of I wish you well,
because love was all I gave
for this pain to hurt like hell.
I'd rather stay heartbroken
because then you'd be to blame
I could be a heartless monster
and then we'd be the same.

But…

Honestly,
I can't blame you
a part of me understands
you're a hurt girl in a hurt world
so, you damage men at every chance
Maybe it's because your father left you
and then your mother found another man
then she went with him, and you were all alone
you never really stood a chance

So...

As much as I'd like to be angry,
resent you and be bitter
I'm afraid I'll have to take the higher road
I'm going to have to be bigger
I hope one day you can love,
and love heals the hurt inside
I'd rather you be happy
than to stay broken inside

Lie to me
one more time
so I don't have to get over you.

Lie with me
one last time
so I don't have to be alone.

Let's just pause time
and stay here
so I don't have to let you go.

Vernajh Pinder

Give me one good reason
why should I stay
and lie down here with you.
Yet, I won't stay
because I'm not optional
and you don't have any options

I hurt myself playing hide and seek with

the concept that you and I

would ever be real

I knew very well I was too good for you,

and you would never measure up

to the love that I needed.

I think sometimes we become so dependent on these false realities we create for ourselves. These alternate worlds where everything is perfect and nothing can go wrong. It is crazy how we do this, knowing we live in an imperfect world. In a world where with each breath we take, something can go awry at any moment. Is it because we crave such perfection that we fail to realize that their beauty is in the imperfections? It's in flaws. It's in every "imperfect" thing that surrounds us. Once we change our perception of what we want to find perfect, I believe we can finally live our lives in happiness.

As you pack your bags
and I usher you out of my life,
I can't help but feel a release
as I get rid of the one toxic thing
that was holding me back from
loving once again.
Now, I exhale.

Vernajh Pinder

Realistically, I think
I allowed thoughts of you
to linger too long.
Or maybe I held on too long
because it was easier for me
and it is always our preference
to do what is easy
Today, at this moment,
I release myself
and with that, I release
the power you had over me.
This is goodbye, forever.

The idea of you
was like love to me.
So, in reality
the "love" I thought existed
was merely
an escape that I created,
I spent all my time
trying not to be alone
only to end up being lonely
in the arms of someone else.
Oh, how we've misconstrued love.

Vernajh Pinder

Some days I wished
I stayed with you
so that I'd never understand
what real love is.

Perfectly, imperfect; Mr. Perfect

my name reminds no matter what I do; it's never

going to be worth it

because no matter how hard I try, it's never utterly

perfect.

That's why I remind myself that

I am the perfectly, imperfect; Mr. Perfect

Vernajh Pinder

Thinking about you made the quintessence of my being covet you. It sought out and captured flattery because you kept feeding the gluttonous nature that was my ego. I said I desired meaningless encounters yet; what I craved was intimacy. I wanted to be held, to be liked, I wanted to be loved. Nevertheless, the only constitutive thing that you desired was me. You coveted my body, my mind, my soul. Parts of me, I wasn't able to fully comprehend. Yet, you hid away from me. That way, it would be easier for you to pull strings. Bit by bit, piece by piece, slowly stealing fragments of me that would never fit together the same way again. My brokenness became a temporary nirvana for you. I should have chosen love, but instead, I went with my deepest desires. I thought to lust after you would be more comfortable than loving you, but I stare back at a cracked reflection debating otherwise. Now my soul lies, where you sole lied because I wanted soul ties, and today I cry. I let the river flow and walk across the water, searching for myself because I lost myself again when I started craving you.

Laying peacefully, yearning for your warmth
in this empty bed.
Reflecting on each time you'd hold me,
or is this all in my head?

I crave your touch,
the way you made me feel.
The late nights cuddling,
 but now what's the deal?

It seems like yesterday
we were happily in love,
now each time I roll over now
I realize I lost my friend.

We made mistakes.
I thought these were things we could work through.
My empty bed is not the same without you.

Vernajh Pinder

The One That Got Away – A short story

Tonight was a stormy night. The wind howled outside, and as the raindrops fell, it sounded like a pitter-patter. Lightning ripped across the sky, and the thunder that followed was deafening. I drew the curtains back as I headed to the kitchen to fetch myself a glass of water. As if the night couldn't get any worse, I stubbed my toe on the bookshelf and watched as a pile of books tumbled to the floor. "Shit', I whispered under my breath. "Mom, are you okay?" My daughter Valerie called out from the bedroom. I screamed back yes and reached down to pick the books up and return them to their proper place on the shelf. Once completed, I went to the kitchen and scrimmaged through the refrigerator for something to drink. It was so many options, but I settled on homemade iced tea. I grabbed a glass out of the cabinet and poured myself a cup before grabbing a seat at the island. I almost jump out of my skin as I feel a tugging on the back of my shirt. It was my Valerie, and she had what looked to be an old photo in her hand. As my eyes focused on the photo, it was a photo of her dad and me. I picked her up and put her in my lap as we both looked at the photo. Vernon was such an amazing father to Valerie, and it's just sad he and I didn't work out. He was a successful hotelier, restaurateur, and hotel consultant and was currently in Europe, closing a deal to open another 5-star boutique hotel in Amsterdam. "I miss daddy," she said, and I could hear the crack in her voice. I wrapped my arms around her, pulling her in for a hug, and whispered, "I do too." Saying those words cut deep like a knife. It's been five years, but the wound still hadn't healed. Each time I thought about it, the wound would reopen itself. Five years ago, I let a good thing, probably the best thing I ever had, get away from me. Valerie's dad, Vernon, and I were engaged to be married. He had a crush on me for what felt like forever, since high school. Vernon was open, so he always told me how he felt, but at the time, I wanted to explore other options.

He was kind, sweet, gentle, and super thoughtful. Honestly, I should have just gotten with him from the jump, but I didn't think I was ready. I explained this to him, and his response was, "it's okay, I am willing to wait for you," and that was what happened. He went off to school and opened his first restaurant. About eight years later, we ended up running into each other at a bar. We went out several more times after that, and eventually, we started dating. After two years, we got engaged, and before I knew it, I was pregnant. Soon after that, we welcomed our beautiful daughter, Valerie, into the world. You would have thought everything would be beautiful after that, but it wasn't'. It all felt like it was going too fast. An old ex, Jordan, reached out to me and said that he was sorry for everything he'd done and wanted to know if I wanted to try again. Then, just like clockwork, my life slowly began to unravel. I couldn't stop thinking about everything he and I use to have but, Vernon was perfect. I didn't want perfect. He was a good father, a good fiancé, a good friend, and a confidant. He was my rock, my everything. Now though, it was beginning to seem like it wasn't enough. One evening after dinner, I explained the situation to Vernon. I repeatedly apologized to him because I was so conflicted. A panged looked crossed into his eyes for a brief second, and then just as quickly as it came, it disappeared. At that moment, I honestly felt like I died 1,000 deaths. Like I couldn't move and was drowning in a pool of my blood. After what felt like an eternity, he finally spoke. "You have to make whatever decision you feel is right at the end of the day," he said. "We built such a great thing, but if you think that you should leave, then I don't want to be the one to stop you from your greatness." I can't even say I was shocked by his response. He never got angry, never raised his voice or his hands. He continued, "I love you with every ounce of being in my body, but if you chase the moon, it's a possibility you lose the sun." He chuckled as he watched the confusion danced across my face. I didn't understand the analogy. He sighed and said, "The moon gives light, but not all the time. Sometimes the light of the moon is temporary.' I nodded as he continued. "The sun, however, although it only shines light during the day. Its light is more potent than that of the moon.

So, while both shine beautiful lights onto the earth, one radiates and lasts longer than the other." Finally, understanding his analogy, I replied, "I want the moon. Do you think the sun would mind?' He looked me deep in my eyes. It felt like he was searching the depths of my soul. In a gentle voice, he said, "The sun waited on the earth before; it's a possibility it won't be any sunshine when you get back." He was earnest when he said it, but I, being the gambler that I am, decided to risk it all. So, I left the sun for the moon and realized the moon's light wasn't even remotely satisfying. I genuinely believed that the sun would still be shining when I came back. Unfortunately, the sun was gone, and there were no chances of getting it to shine its light on me again. I still regret it to this day that I let the sun be the one that got away.

I was so interested in you,
never understanding that
my sole interest wasn't because
my soul was interested in you.
I was complicit in indoctrinating
this false belief of what our love was,
or merely of what you needed it to be.
The idea of me loving you
was a better belief
as opposed to me going through
with loving you.
I just wanted to peel off the layers
because I just wanted to lay up in you.
It was your beauty that made me hysterical
and each minute away from you unbearable.
You see, I never cared for you
I just wanted to peek into your treasure
as we simultaneously reached our peak.
My only goal was my pleasure.
The mind was interested, but my heart? Never...

Vernajh Pinder

The ocean washed the façade away
and with it,
any lingering thoughts of you.
The crashing waves disseminated them,
and it was then
that I finally realized
you were never there from the start.

The moon bathed me in hope,

my mind drenched

with thoughts of you.

The stars chanted your name

over and over again,

leaving me stuck in a trance.

There is no getting over you,

is there?

Did your father never love you?
Did your brothers never protect you?
How could you dare call it love
and be with a man who disrespects you?

Did your mother never say you're beautiful?
Is that why you search within his eyes?
As he strips you of your innocence,
submerged in the web of lies.

Was your sister not your role model,
showing you the elegance of life?
You let him cut your confidence into pieces
using words and not a knife.

I pray one day you cut
the strings that he's attached.
Finding someone to love you unconditionally,
unlocking the heart that you've latched.

Vernajh Pinder

He stood there in silence,
looking into the fire that blazed,
holding the letter he never sent.
It's words describing everything you ever meant

His fingers seemed to have a mind of their own
because although his brain was saying to hold it,
he saw the paper sliding gently in the breeze
and watched keen-eyed as its ashes floating into
trees.

He watched as every painful memory of you
dissipated into nothingness.
Each moment eviscerated from his heart,
the torment from when it all fell apart

In the end, he did what was necessary.
As his last memories of you evaporated,
the beauty of it went.
Burned away in the letter never sent.

Self-love is a journey, not a destination. Anyone that tries to tell you otherwise has not mastered it yet. It is an ongoing process that continually challenges you to push beyond your comfort zone. Only then, when you can move past the boundaries and limits set, will you be able to offer love to someone else.

Vernajh Pinder

His idea of love
was distorted by
false realities and fairytales.
Love was messy.
It was a beautiful tragedy
and he wanted
all parts of it.

Hope You Don't Get Famous

I hope the moon kicks you
and the sun laughs,
but I hope you get those flowers
I sent on my behalf.

I hope your days are dark
and your nights are haunting,
but I hope you find love
because that's all you've been wanting.

I hope time speeds up for you
and leaves you broken,
but I hope you travel the world
seizing every moment.

I sometimes hope you suffer,
and you don't know why.
I hope you find someone
to dry the tears from your eyes.

You see, a part of me loves you
and wishes you nothing but the best.
Still, it's a part of me that is broken
and it hopes your whole life is a mess.

So…

I hope one day you're happy
and there is no bad blood between us
Until that day and time,
I hope you don't get famous.

I wish one day you find love
because your heart has broken many times.
You've been taken for granted,
and granted you've given him another chance to
cross the line.

I wish one day you heal
and mend that aching soul.
Finding the courage to take care of yourself
will eventually make you whole.

I wish you would let me help you,
carry the burden of the pain.
Sometimes broken is beautiful,
so let me stand with you in the rain.

I wish one day you stand tall,
and your crown may tilt but never falls.
Let me be your King and you, my Queen.
Together we can conquer it all.

Vernajh Pinder

I spent too much time
on hating you.
I spent all my time
writing you as the villain,
when you were not.
You were just someone
trying to figure out
what you wanted
and what you deserved.
So, I can't be mad at you
for doing something
I would have done myself.

Sometimes we think it's easier to love certain parts of people, scared to say aloud who or what they are. As humans, I think it is because we tend only to want to love the pleasant parts. Therefore, we let the bad parts fester like a sore. We must allow the hourglass to run out of sand because real, unconditional love is like watching a baby breathing its first breath. It is innocent. It is beautiful. This absurd idea we concocted that love hurts is nothing more than an idea. A diversion to avert your gaze from the truth, that love is painless.

The Final Letter

To whom this may concern:

It is disheartening to know that our good times have arrived at their final scene. When I reflect on the moments we have created together; it breaks my heart that it wasn't our time. I fought tooth and nail to be with you, but it always seemed as though you had other intentions.

I was willing to risk it all. Hell, I would have sold my soul if that meant we could be together. It is unfortunate how we always want the things that we can't have or just simply aren't designed for us. Allowing the false notions to consume us, never realizing the startling truth right before our eyes: that sometimes opposites don't attract, they merely push each other further apart.

The pain of heartbreak sometimes is so devastating that our brain plays tricks on us. It doesn't want us to truly feel that pain, so it blocks it out, so the heart doesn't have to live through it. The truth hurts, but sometimes it's easier to believe the story of what we could have been instead of what we are not. The thought of never being with you feels like I'm sinking deep into the arctic ocean, slowly becoming hypothermic.

In the end, I think I should be whole than to be broken into the pieces that loving you would bring. With that, I think I have finally realized that you were not the one for me, and it's okay. No matter the number of years we invested in each other, it was toxic for both of us. The scars you left on my heart will heal eventually, and the pain that I may have caused you will ultimately dissipate. Maybe, we can be examples that it is possible to start over and find love again. We don't have to be the victims of our previous relationships; we will be able to love once again.

As you take the time you need to heal, I just ask that whoever comes your way you treat them with dignity and respect. I want you to allow yourself to be vulnerable. Not everyone will hurt you. Some people choose to love you; you need to give them a chance. Before today, I never would have said this, but I genuinely hope you do get famous.

Best Regards,
Your former lover

Hope You Don't Get Famous

As sure as

the sun shines

during the day,

and the moon

kisses the sky at night,

love will find us all eventually.

You just have to patient

because love will always prevail.

About the author

Vernajh Pinder is a poet from the Bahamas. He is an avid reader, lover of poetry, music, art, food, and wine. He graduated from the University of Maryland Eastern Shore with a Bachelor of Science in Hospitality and Tourism Management. To keep up to date with his work, you can find him on Instagram as @vernthepoet.

Made in the USA
Middletown, DE
28 April 2023

29587737R00091